A SIXTY-MINUTE GUIDE TO
DISRUPTION

PRAISE FOR THE DARK SIDE OF INNOVATION

Chopra has produced an 'owner's manual' for addressing disruption. A must read!

- Len Schlesinger,
President Emeritus-Babson College,
formerly COO of Limited Brand

Professor Chopra provides a practical process on how to deal with disruptive innovation, and even how to thrive in the face of such dramatic change. Ignore the lessons at your own peril!

- Peter Corijn
Vice President P&G

Disruptive innovations are going at businesses at an ever faster rate. Prof. Chopra's book will serve as a lighthouse in stormy seas for business leaders across the industry spectrum. An easy read, equal in incisive thought and real-world examples. A great investment of my time.

- Jaideep Mehta
Vice President, IDC

You have tapped into some very interesting insights. Your book is also very rich in examples which help to really strengthen your message. You provide compelling evidence that should be a wake-up call in many contexts.

- Paul Geoffrey Jeremaes
HP Innovation Centers

This book is perfect for a workshop every company should do once every 2-3 years, if not more often.

- Prof. Abhijit Guha
Assistant Professor of Marketing,
Wayne State University

A SIXTY-MINUTE GUIDE TO
DISRUPTION

A SURVIVAL GUIDE IN THE AGE OF DISRUPTION

PROMETHEAN
STRATEGIES

A Sixty-Minute Guide to Disruption

Cover and Book Design: Biljana Dabic

ISBN: 978-0-9986081-1-2

Promethean Strategies
4 S Orange Ave #306, South Orange,
New Jersey 07079

This book is dedicated to all innovators who are searching for high impact opportunities.

CONTENTS

INTRODUCTION

The art of managing disruption is quickly becoming a critical tool for managers across industries. You can add significant value to your career by building this capability. This book will help you take an important step in this direction.

Disruption is a fascinating phenomenon. When a large established company fails, it is a major event. It also has significant consequences for employees, customers, partners, industry and the country.

Take the originator of mass photography as an example. When Kodak failed, it was not just a big event in the camera industry; it had ripple effects on many companies. The entire community in the headquarters location in Rochester, New York, suffered.

Why This Book?

You have probably chosen this book because of your interest in understanding disruption. You've seen it work when large firms fail and perhaps you've wondered if this can happen to any business - including yours. It's worth making the investment to understand disruption because there is a method to predict it.

I was in the same position as you - I was fascinated by this phenomenon and intrigued by its multiple facets. I wanted to understand it in depth. As a result, I spent almost a decade studying disruption. I have learned quite a lot from my own research on hundreds of companies as well as benefited from the research of thousands of other researchers on this topic.

> **❝** This book will give you a rich understanding of disruption in 60 minutes.

I wrote this book because I wanted to share what I have learned in a condensed format. It will give you the answers you seek, supported by years of reading research by thousands of researchers. It will give you a deeper understanding of disruption and the tools to manage it. This will allow you to be a step ahead in your career where this skill is fast becoming critical.

The Disruption Management Imperative

Did you know that firms get disrupted for dozens of reasons? A disruptive technology is only one of the many reasons it happens; small and incremental innovations often lead to disruption too.

We are in an unprecedented age of disruption. No industry is immune from these forces. Although quartz technology and digital cameras were disruptive forces, they took decades to materialize. In more recent years, we see many disruptive forces emerge rapidly and without much notice. Moreover, disruptive forces are becoming more prevalent across more industries.

Businesses no longer have the luxury of responding to disruptive forces after those forces become apparent. Firms that respond to disruptive events after they become evident find it difficult to survive. Symbian and Blackberry responded to Apple only after Steve Jobs launched the first iPhone. They didn't have enough time to deliver an effective response.

This age of disruption has created an imperative for companies to create a new capability in disruption management. Only with such a capability can companies anticipate disruptions before they become real. Today's leaders need to be masters of this practice.

You and Disruption

You need to be well equipped with an advanced understanding of the techniques to manage this phenomenon. No matter what role you play in a business organization, you need to master the vocabulary of disruption. It will not only make you a more effective innovator but will also help you add significant value to your business and organization.

"
No matter your role, you need to master the vocabulary of disruption.

This short book will allow you to get a good understanding of disruption in just 60 minutes. Within an hour, you will build enough absorptive capacity of disruption. Whether you want to understand disruptive threats to your business or want to become a disruptor, you will find the needed knowledge in the chapters ahead.

At the end of this book, do spend some time on the section "you and disruption" for some ideas on how to use this knowledge to advance your career. It will also provide you with advise on some of the next steps you can take to continue to build this critical capability.

Enjoy reading the book and building new skills.

CHAPTER I:
WHAT IS DISRUPTION?

Disruption is a widely used word that has different meanings in different contexts. Sometimes this varying usage causes confusion.

Most often, disruption in the business world refers to the displacement of an incumbent firm by another firm (e.g. Apple disrupted Symbian). Joseph Schumpeter was perhaps one of the earliest scholars to work on disruption. His book *Capitalism, Socialism, and Democracy* was first published in 1942. He coined the term "creative destruction" to refer to disruption. In fact, he built his theory on the original works of Karl Marx.

Many people confuse the term disruption with disruptive innovation. In fact, people use the word disruptive in three distinct ways.

Disruption Explained

First and perhaps most commonly, disruption refers to innovation that dislodges an incumbent. Extensive research has shown that disruption can arise due to a number of factors affecting normal business operations. These can range from technological innovation to governmental intervention. The same research shows that it is difficult to predict disruption with certainty. It cannot be declared today that Tesla will disrupt General Motors or that Amazon will disrupt Walmart. Disruption is only known in hindsight, but it is possible to learn and understand the conditions that lead to it.

> **"** Disruption is the displacement of an incumbent firm.

Disruptive Technology – Incorrect Usage

Second (and a common misuse of the term) is to refer to a significant innovation that involves massive change as disruptive. For example, someone may say the smartwatch is a disruptive technology because it uses an entirely different technology than a quartz watch.

When people use the term disruptive to denote a big technological change, they make a mistake. They assume the technological change would result in disruption. This assumption is incorrect because large technological changes do not always lead to disruption. People sometimes use the term to mean major (as opposed to a minor) innovation.

Disruptive Technology – Correct Usage

Third, it refers to a disruptive technology as coined by Clayton Christensen in his book, *Innovator's Dilemma*. In this sense, it relates to innovation that changes the key purchasing criteria of a customer. For example, a mobile phone is a disruptive technology for landline phones because as customers began to value the mobility of a phone, it became a new purchase criterion.

Christensen found that when the key buying criteria change, incumbent firms get disrupted. Other scholars have found evidence that this does not always hold true. As a result, innovation may be disruptive (in Christiansen speak) but may not always disrupt (in Schumpeter speak) an incumbent.

> **" A disruptive technology is a technology that changes the key purchase criteria of customers.**

In spite of the fact that disruptive innovations do not always result in disruption, the research on disruptive innovations is important. It shows some important conditions where dominant firms can be blindsided by an innovation.

Christensen found that sometimes a technology arises that is inferior to the mainstream technology on the key purchase criterion. When this occurs, the core customers of dominant market share companies do not desire that technology. As a result, the incumbents treat it as a non-threat. Often peripheral customers buy into such an emerging technology that mainstream providers have discounted. Over time, this "underdog" technology improves on the features most important to customers. Eventually, the inferior technology surpasses the older technology on the features most important to mainstream customers.

At that point, it offers additional features now matching or surpassing the previously existing mainstream technology. The mainstream customers switch to the new technology — the market is disrupted as the key purchase criteria for the customers changes.

The reason incumbents get disrupted in this situation is that they stop investing in emerging technology once they realize that mainstream customers do not want it. In effect, the incumbents get blindsided and get disrupted.

Christensen found in his research that a disruptive technology (one that changes purchase criterion of customers) led to disruption (the displacement of incumbents) in the hard disk drive industry. It's actually the foundation of his research that led him to connect disruptive technologies with disruption.

Other researchers studied the same industry and found different results. Andrew King and Christopher Tucci studied the hard disk industry and found that although many firms were disrupted due to disruptive technology, many others were not disrupted.

"
> King and Tucci's research showed that not all firms in disk drive industry were disrupted due to a disruptive technology.

There are many examples of situations where a disruptive innovation did not lead to disruption. Mobile search is an excellent example. When Apple brought apps to mobile devices, people began to use that instead of internet search. However, Google did not get disrupted. Instead, Google emerged even more dominant in mobile search.

The Cause of Confusion

This confusion between disruption and disruptive innovation has misinformed many students and managers. The assumption that all disruption takes place due to disruptive innovations is not true. Similarly, not all disruptive innovations disrupt incumbents. This was at the core of the **scathing attack by New Yorker on Christensen's work**.

In my opinion, the problem is not with Christensen's work but with how people interpreted it. When people started confusing disruptive technologies with disruption, they made a mistake. As long as you understand that disruptive technologies only sometimes lead to disruption you will not make the same mistake.

The key reason why people make this mistake is that they confused cause and effect because of similar terminology. This error is akin to saying everything juicy eventually becomes a juice and assuming that all juices come from something juicy.

Similarly, people assumed that every disruptive technology will lead to disruption.

In fact, by categorizing every major innovation as a disruptive innovation, this mistake is often magnified.

What Causes Failure of Firms?

For over 80 years, thousands of researchers have studied this phenomenon. Sociologists, economists, and organizational theorist have researched it from countless angles. Disruptive technology is a property of technological change that can sometimes cause disruption - but it does not always cause disruption. More importantly, there are dozens of other reasons for disruption.

In my research, I studied how a profit destroying innovation can cause an incumbents displacement. I found that firms find it hard to respond to such innovations and get disrupted. But many times, companies do create solutions against profit destroying inventions and continue to survive. I have written about profit destroying innovations in my book *The Dark Side of Innovation* as well as in my award winning paper *Deer in the headlights: Response of incumbent firms to profit destroying innovations.*

Survival Versus Disruption

To me, what is most interesting is how a firm can survive for decades in spite of facing many disruptive forces.

I find it impressive that after 80 years of research on disruption, scholars have not been able to identify a single cause that will guarantee disruption. This to me is a testament to the intelligence, creativity, and grit of managers across millions of firms.

> **"** What is most interesting is how a firm can survive for decades in spite of facing many disruptive forces.

A big takeaway for you should be that no matter how big a disruptive force you face, there is no guarantee that your business will get disrupted by it. It is in your power to succeed against the strongest disruptive forces in the world.

Thinking About Disruption

Once you understand that disruption is a much bigger phenomenon than disruptive technologies, it opens a Pandora's box. Many questions arise due to this understanding. Some of them are as follows:

What causes disruption?
Can it be avoided?
Are more firms being disrupted today?
Am I safe from disruption?
How can I ensure my business does not get disrupted?

Senior leaders in every company are asking these questions. Some are asking this after being threatened by disruptive forces while others are worried that their business may get disrupted.

This creates an opportunity for you. By learning the art of managing disruption, you can create value for your company and business.

♀ CHAPTER INSIGHT:

Disruption is a displacement of a dominant firm. Disruptive innovation refers to an innovation that changes purchasing criterion in a market. Disruptive innovations do not always lead to disruption. Not all disruptions take place due to disruptive innovations.

CHAPTER II:
THE TWO MAIN CAUSES OF DISRUPTION

Although disruption has been a buzzword for the last few years, economists and sociologists have been studying it for decades. In the eight decades since Schumpeter's book was published, thousands of scholars have worked on understanding disruption. They found dozens of reasons why firms get disrupted. Other than my own research on survival, I went through thousands of books and research articles to grasp why firms fail.

The Root Cause of Disruption

Although there are dozens of reasons why firms get disrupted, they essentially boil down to a single reason: firms fail because they are unable to respond to a change in their environment.

Firms are often called upon to adapt in two ways. First, firms need to *innovate* to stay relevant in their market. As an example, car companies continue to launch new models every year in order to stay relevant. This is the first order adaptation that firms need to make on an ongoing basis. If they do not innovate, they fall behind and can get disrupted.

"

Firms fail because they are unable to respond to a change in their environment.

Second, sometimes firms need to *transform* themselves in order to stay relevant. For instance, when the digital cameras began to replace film roll cameras, Kodak and Polaroid needed to transform themselves into electronics and hardware firms in order to stay relevant. Transformation is a second order adaptation where firms need to make changes in the way they are. It involves not just a change in their products but also fundamental changes in the way they operate.

When firms fail in either innovation or transformation, they get disrupted.

A Car Race Analogy

Let us understand the relationship between disruption, innovation, and transformation using an analogy of a hypothetical car race.

The Rules

Imagine you are participating in a car race where the rules are as follows. After each round, the last three cars are eliminated from the contest. The remaining cars continue to the next round. Once disqualified, a car cannot come back to the race. A new car can always join the race, but it needs to complete the previous rounds and catch up with current participants. As the contest continues, new cars stop joining the race as the distance to be covered becomes too great to close. The winners are decided when the relative positions of the racers do not change for many rounds.

The last rule is that prior to the race, you need to choose one car that you will drive as your race car. Once you choose a car, you have to stick with that choice until the end of the race or until you are eliminated.

The Role of Innovation in Car Race

If you were a participant in such a race, you would likely ensure that you find ways to remain ahead of the other participants using many means. You could use superior technology, better skills or even use smart tactics to stay ahead of the race.

" This car race analogy shows the relationship between innovation, transformation and disruption.

You may learn how tire pressure leads to better handling and thus maintain the right pressure. You could even tweak your engine to make it more powerful. Each time you use these measures to stay ahead of the competition, you are using innovation to win the game.

If you did nothing while your competition innovated, you would soon slip to the bottom of the list and be eliminated. This is how companies who do not innovate against their competition get disrupted.

Rules Change

Now, let's assume that the rules of game change. The car race moves beyond a race track to natural settings. You are now supposed to travel over busy streets, dirt roads and across mountain paths. To be able to remain in the race, you still need to finish each round without ranking in the bottom three positions.

This shift in rules of the game requires that you are able to transform your car to do things that most cars cannot do. This time, you need to be agile at slow speeds on city streets.

You now need durability and adequate suspension on dirt tracks. You are also required to fly over water and zip around mountains because the new cars joining the race have these abilities. If you are unable to make these needed adjustments, you will not remain in the race.

A Call for Transformation

Due to new competitors and new terrains, you are now required to transform your car into a space age vehicle that can do things that normal cars cannot do.

At this stage if you wish to get a modern car with better capabilities in place of your old car, you are out of luck. The rules of the game state that you cannot change your car. So the only option open to you is to transform your car.

Car Analogy in Real Life

When the rules of the game change in an industry, firms are often required to transform themselves. If firms fail to adjust, they end up being disrupted. This happens because they either fail to innovate or fail to transform themselves when needed.

Blackberry had to innovate in order to compete with Apple, but it was unsuccessful in matching the user experience of the iPhone. This threat is very real to all businesses. Many firms fail to innovate commensurately and thus get disrupted. The needed innovations are not always major innovations. Sometimes they are small innovations. (Surprising examples of disruption by minor innovation are given in a later chapter).

Very often companies are required to transform themselves. Kodak was a chemical company that needed to become a hardware company. Sony is a hardware company that needed to transform itself into a software and hardware company.

Sometimes, new competitors just have a much better fit with the environment. They are akin to cars that can fly when your car cannot. For example. Southwest Airlines was much more agile than Delta due to its structure. At such times, companies may recognize that a transformation is needed, but find it a very difficult process to undertake.

Going Beyond This Chapter

This chapter summarized the key reason why firms get disrupted. But there is a lot more to it. There are reasons why firms fail to innovate and adapt to their environment. Understanding these reasons will help you really get to the bottom of this puzzle: Why do firms fail to innovate even when their life depends on innovation?

To keep this book's promise of being a sixty minute read, I have not included details that deal with structural barriers to innovation. In fact, there is a lot more to failure of firms than what I have covered in this short guide. You can delve deeper into disruption with my premier courses on managing disruption at my online academy.

At the academy, you will find numerous resources that will help you become a more informed busines leader.

You can get more details on the academy at http://ankush-chopra.com

💡CHAPTER INSIGHT:

What is the call to action for your firm? Innovation or transformation? What are the hurdles you face in your path today?

CHAPTER III:
THE NIGHTMARE SCENARIO OF DISRUPTION

If you are a large company with strong brands and a dominant industry position, you are secure. You are a Goliath with deep pockets and a small business upstart can be no match for you. There is a lot of evidence to support this view. For example, consider Comcast and Verizon as the Goliaths in the cable industry. They faced a threat from a small company named Tivo, which developed a new Digital Video Recorder (DVR). Users loved Tivo, following it with their hearts and pockets. But in the end, the big cable guys continued to do well whereas Tivo made no money.

Although many such stories exist, there is bad news for Goliaths. Every Goliath has a psychological chink in his armor that makes him vulnerable. When someone hits this chink, Goliath will fall.

The Chink in Goliath's Armor

This chink in Goliath's armor appears when he faces a particular set of choices. When he has to choose between an innovation that reduces profits and the status quo, he makes bad decisions. Although the rational behavior would be to take the lesser of the two evils (live with a lower profit), he resists this path. In doing so, he exposes the psychological chink in his armor that can stun him into inactivity. This is what I have termed the Dark Side of Innovation. I researched this and wrote about this phenomenon in my first book *The Dark Side Of Innovation*.

> **"** Every Goliath has a psychological chink in his armor that makes him vulnerable? When someone hits this chink, Goliath will fall.

The Story of Vanguard

Vanguard exploited this chink in Goliath's armor to rise from being a small and unknown company to being a leader in the mutual fund industry. It faced Goliaths such as Fidelity and State Street in a mature industry and succeeded.

Before 1975, all mutual funds were active funds. The fund managers would trade securities to beat their particular benchmark index, such as S&P 500. The belief was that if you have better research and can get in-and-out of the market at the right times, you could be ahead of the index. For this strategy, fund managers used to charge high management fees. The business was quite lucrative.

Vanguard's CEO Jack Bogle found something surprising. The funds that aimed to beat the index most often failed to do so. This occurred because of two reasons. First, active management did not deliver consistent superior returns. Second, the high fees that funds charged their clients lowered returns for the investors. Active management was a fool's errand; however, nobody had thought of that until Bogle had this epiphany. He offered a better solution: why not just buy the entire index (and hold it). This would provide index returns without high management fees. His promise yielded 80% lower fees on index funds.

The Response of Incumbents

This path spelled disaster for bigger investment houses. If they followed Bogle and converted their funds to index holdings, that would reduce their revenues by over 80%. If they didn't follow the innovation and investors were swayed towards index funds, they may lose a lot of business. Their choice was to embrace a profit destroying innovation or ignore it.

" They didn't believe anyone would buy such a poor product that offers 'average' performance. And in doing so, they exposed their psychological chink that made them underestimate the power of Vanguard.

They not only ignored it but also berated Bogle for what they termed "the mediocrity" he was peddling. They didn't believe anyone would buy such a poor product that offers 'average' performance. And in doing so, they exposed their psychological chink as they underestimated the power of the dark side of innovation. As a result, when Vanguard offered index funds, competitors did not follow. This allowed Vanguard to succeed, becoming the new leader in the industry.

The Prevalence of the Dark Side of Innovation

Although the index fund example may appear to be a unique case, you will be surprised how often profit destroying innovations appear on the horizon. Quartz watches were profit destroying for mechanical watches.

For hundreds of years, the Swiss watchmakers had built the best capabilities in watchmaking. They had developed intricate knowledge of building mechanical components needed in a watch. This helped them maintain a dominant position in the industry.

However, quartz watch technology eliminated the need for that intricate knowledge. Suddenly, anyone could create a watch as accurate as a Swiss mechanical watch. This led to new competition from the Japanese and American competitors. As a result of this competition, profit margins in the industry fell precipitously.

Swiss watchmakers had two choices. One option was to embrace quartz and lower their own profits. A second consideration was to avoid the technology in the hope that it would not succeed. They chose the latter and the technology succeeded. As a result, over half the Swiss watchmakers disappeared within ten years.

I call this scenario the dark side of innovation because it is a cognitive trap that hides the truth. Companies facing it do not realize that they are underestimating the likelihood of the innovation succeeding. This happens due to some deep biases within human nature. Hundreds of companies have fallen and failed in this situation.

The Lesson

So what is the secret of finding this psychological chink in your armor? You have to be aware of profit-destroying innovations and how companies create them. Vanguard created one by changing a deep-rooted belief in the industry. The belief that you can consistently beat the index was at the heart of the profits of the mutual fund industry. When Bogle assaulted this belief, he created a profit destroying innovation.

> **"** When Bogle assaulted this belief, he created a profit destroying innovation.

Note: I wrote an entire book detailing this phenomenon across hundreds of companies and dozens of industries. I designed a framework to help companies develop innovations or predict potential profit destroying innovations in any industry. I go into considerable detail on the psychological reasons behind the dark side of innovation. If you would like to learn more about profit destroying innovations, please refer to *The Dark Side of Innovation.*

♀ CHAPTER INSIGHT:

Which deep rooted belief holds the key to profits in your industry? Is there a small company trying to change it? If yes, that little guy may eat your lunch and run away with your business.

CHAPTER IV:
UNDERSTANDING THE AGE OF DISRUPTION

We are witnessing an unprecedented era of disruption in the business world. Mobile devices are disrupting conventional computers. E-Commerce is disrupting traditional retail. Fintech is threatening the banking industry. The wave of disruption is sweeping across every industry and is threatening to push incumbents toward oblivion. To survive this age of disruption, you need to understand three powerful trends and know how to deal with them.

This age of disruption is marked by three key trends in the business world.

Increasing Prevalence of Disruptive Forces

In the 1990s, forces of disruption were affecting a handful of industries. Today this effect is pervasive. Uber, Airbnb, VOIP, Netflix and LED are just a few examples of disruptive forces. Even when incumbents survive these disruptions, they still face massive pain.

When taxi drivers in cities around the world went on strike against the rise of Uber, it was their response to the pain caused by this disruptive event in their industry. When hotels in New York and Boston started to lobby the government against AirBnB, it was because of the pain they also felt due to a disruptive force.

> **"** Disruptive threats used to be a once-a-century event. It is now becoming common across industries.

In the past, companies in consumer staples with rock-solid brands were immune to disruption. This is no longer the case. Consider the example of a small unknown company like Dollar Shave Club (DSC). It came out of nowhere and grabbed a nontrivial share of the shave care market. DSC did this in the presence of an 800-ton Gorilla: Gillette.

It seems that no industry is immune from disruptive forces anymore.

Increasing Speed of Disruptive Events

It took 30 years for digital cameras to disrupt analog cameras and 15 years for quartz watches to disrupt mechanical watches. But, it took five years for iPhone to displace Symbian and Blackberry.

If Facebook was a country, it would be the largest nation in the world. Facebook has 1.65 billion users. It was born in 2004, just 12 years ago. Dropbox, Spotify and Airbnb were born in 2008 and Uber in 2009. All these companies have had a major impact on the incumbents in different industries. The young age of these companies tells the story of the increasing speed of disruptive forces.

> **"** Facebook has 1.65 billion users. It was born in 2004, just 12 years ago.

I meet leaders in old companies who are amazed at the speed at which the world is moving today. This causes a massive pain (meaning slowing growth, lower profits, layoffs and other pressures) to companies who are used to a slower pace in the world.

Older companies are being forced to deal with the issue of speed. Although speed became a critical issue in the late 1990s, most firms have had little experience with the speed of change in the market they are facing today.

Logitech makes keyboards and accessories for the mobile devices, among many other products. When Apple launches a new iPad, it doesn't inform Logitech in advance as it is a competitor with its complementary products. Logitech needs to build accessories for new mobile devices soon after such products are launched. Many other new competitors are emerging against Logitech today. Speed has indeed become a critical success factor for the accessories industry. When a consumer buys the new iPad and needs a cover or an external keyboard, if a Logitech keyboard is not yet available, the chance to sell to that customer is lost until the next upgrade cycle. As a result, Logitech spent enormous resources on increasing speed to market for its accessories.

Speed of business has been increasingly becoming a critical measure across the world. Procter & Gamble undertook a massive transformation effort called Organization 2005 to improve it speed to market. With the new structure, it hoped to take its innovations to the market faster.

Although companies have dealt with speed related issues for many years, the speed of events today is unparalleled. Old companies are not used to these speeds and this lack of experience makes them somewhat more vulnerable.

There are several reasons why the speed of disruptive events has increased which are detailed in the next chapter.

Many Disruptive Threats per Industry

How many tectonic shifts did a typical industry face in the 20th century? The camera industry, watch industry and the mutual fund industry faced one disruption each. Today, in the 21st century, many industries face more than one such major event.

Watch makers have already seen two disruptive events since the turn of the century. First, mobile devices reduced demand for watches. Second, smart watches are trying to take over the wrist real estate.

Likewise, the financial services industry is being inundated with many disruptive threats coming from the fintech wave; the insurance industry is witnessing nine disruptive events.

Speed of Response in the Age of Disruption

The speed, prevalence and force of disruptive events are overwhelming even for the strongest firms. These forces are eroding the competitive advantage of successful companies, making them vulnerable to future shocks. As a result, even the most successful companies face an uncertain future.

"

> The increasing speed of disruptions needs a lightening fast response from incumbents.

The increasing speed of disruptions needs a lightening fast response from incumbents. Kodak had over 20 years to respond to the digital challenge and Swiss Watchmakers had ten years to respond to the quartz challenge. Those longer time spans appear to be a luxury compared to the time companies have today to respond to disruption.

Strategic Imperative in the Age of Disruption

Today, there are more undiscovered threats than in any previous era. Companies do not have the luxury of waiting for a disruption to arrive before reacting. You need to have a befitting response ready even before a disruption arrives on your horizon.

Above all, recognizing that there are increased threats means that you need to build capabilities in disruption management. With such capabilities, you will be able to predict potential disruptions before they arrive. You can be proactive rather than reactive. Disruption management capabilities will allow you to track the forces of disruption rather than be surprised by them. Finally, these capabilities will help you design a broader set of response options than you do today.

"
> You need to build capabilities in disruption management.

💡 CHAPTER INSIGHT:

What is your company doing today to survive in the age of disruption?

CHAPTER V:
UNDERSTANDING THE FORCES DRIVING THE AGE OF DISRUPTION

In the previous chapter, we learned the three hallmarks of the age of disruption. In this chapter, I will detail what is driving this age of disruption. This will help us identify whether these trends are an abnormality or the initial marking of a new normal?

I have identified three primary drivers responsible for ushering in the age of disruption. First, network based economic models are responsible for increasing the speed of disruptive events. Second, the Internet (as a great leveler) creates conditions for greater prevalence of multiple disruptive events. Third, increasing wealth inequality is fueling disruptive events.

Network Economics Based Business Models

When you buy a product such as a toothpaste, the value you derive from it is entirely from the toothpaste. But when you purchase a telephone, you derive a lot more value from the total user base of phones. If you had the most sophisticated phone in the world but you were the only user, it would be worthless to you. In other words, the total value of a product consists of value from the product and the value from the user base.

This segregation of value tells you whether network economics is at work in an industry. The greater the value from the user base as a part of the total value from a product, the higher the network economics. Using this model, the toothpaste business has no network economics, but the telephone industry has high network economics.

> **❝** It is like a virtuous cycle where more people using a product makes the product more valuable. So more people use it, and so on.

Consider companies like Ebay, Facebook, Google and WhatsApp. The common theme among them is the extent of network economics at play. Many new business models have high network economics. If only 50 people used Uber, it is almost worthless to either drivers or riders. But as an increasing number of people use the service, it becomes more valuable to both the drivers and passengers.

If you have studied basic economics but not studied network economics, it is because this is an advanced concept as well as a more recent phenomenon. Network based economic models are a reflection of the new world.

Research has shown that winners will take all of the market in a network economics environment. It is like a virtuous cycle where more people using a product makes the product more valuable, so more people use it, and so on.

In network economics, the speed of adoption should also increase as more people adopt a product or service. Although Uber started in 2009, in less than seven years its valuation exceeded $65 billion.

The Internet as a Great Leveler

The Internet has democratized access to markets, supply base and technology to a great extent. It has driven down the marginal cost of communication to zero - a message to one person or one to a million people costs the same. It has also enabled enormous interconnectedness. These factors have quashed the old entry barriers across industries that existed at one time.

In the previous century, if a new entrant had to enter the shave care business, it was pretty much impossible. Shelf space and access to distribution network itself were significant barriers. But today, Dollar Shave Club has taken over eight percent of this market in only a few years. It developed a creative message, a new business model and reached millions. It did this without a distribution network. The internet allowed it to access millions of users at a low cost. Social media, built upon the enormous interconnectedness, has enabled market access at viral speeds.

"
These factors have quashed the old entry barriers across industries.

Today, you can access skilled freelancers on the internet irrespective of where you are based. It is now possible to hire a designer, a coder, an editor or a video producer in a few hours. The information asymmetry and access asymmetry are things of the past.

Technology is being democratized. Where once an expensive studio was needed to produce content, today only an iPhone is necessary. Instead of an expensive darkroom, a photoshop program costing a few dollars a month accomplishes the same goals today.

The Internet has leveled the business world to a great extent. A startup can access millions of consumers quickly and at low costs. It can obtain superior skills in a very short timeframe and without upfront investment. It can also obtain superior technologies at low costs. Many traditional advantages of large established firms are dwindling.

That means a small company (such as Dollar Shave Club) can become an overnight sensation now.

This is fueling greater prevalence of disruptive events and yielding the emergence of multiple disruptive events in a single industry.

Increasing Wealth Inequality

It is common knowledge that wealth inequality is increasing and wealth is becoming concentrated with fewer people. Such wealth seeks sophisticated investment strategies undertaken by venture capital and private equity. Venture capital and private equity seek higher risk investments for significant payoffs.

Such investment managers are more likely to fund major disruptive ideas than incremental and safe ideas. This burgeoning wealth has been chasing an increasing number of disruptive opportunities. Concentrated wealth seeking disruptive investment ideas also explains the growing prevalence of disruptive ideas in so many industries.

"

> This burgeoning wealth has been chasing an increasing number of opportunities for disruptive business ideas.

It is ironic that senior managers investing in venture capital are funding disruptive ideas. These same ideas are coming back to haunt their own businesses.

♀CHAPTER INSIGHT:

How many of these three factors do you recognize at play in your industry?

CHAPTER VI:
HOW SHOULD YOU THINK ABOUT DISRUPTION

When you think of disruption, you may imagine companies like Kodak and Polaroid going bankrupt. However, when Android took over the leadership position from iOS, it was not a disruption. As a result, it is natural for you to think of disruption as a binary event. Either a firm gets disrupted or not.

This binary thinking is dangerous and will cost you a lot in your career as well as in business. It will make you take bigger risks than you realize.

Massive Pain Without Disruption

Businesses sometimes face a disruptive force but still survive. Index fund innovation is a great example. This invention helped Vanguard rise from a peripheral position to a leadership position of the industry. Nevertheless, as it *displaced* Fidelity and State Street as leaders, it did not disrupt them.

Although Fidelity did not get disrupted, Vanguard forced it to cut asset management fees. If you have been in a situation where you had to keep cutting prices, you know it is quite painful.

As I mentioned in the previous chapters, Dollar Shave Club is a disruptive force in the shave care market. But it has only taken eight percent of the market share, and it is unlikely that it would come even close to disrupting Gillette. But losing even five percentage points for a Goliath is a significant pain.

Take the case of two new businesses based on sharing excess capacity. Uber and AirBNB allow owners of assets to monetize excess capacity. Uber is unlikely to significantly disrupt the taxi industry anytime soon. AirBNB is unlikely to disrupt the hotel industry. Nevertheless, they have caused massive pain to millions of hotels and taxi companies.

"

These examples show that even when a disruptive force does not disrupt, it can cause huge pain.

These examples show that even when a disruptive force does not disrupt, it can cause huge pain. This pain ensues because disruptive forces create excess capacity and force structural adjustments. Such changes include a permanent loss of some profit and layoffs. Moreover, they force you to change how you do business.

Disruptive Forces

A force that pushes a firm towards disruption is a disruptive force. These include many competitive, environmental, socio-economic and behavioral changes.

For example, cutting the cord has been a trend in the US economy for many years. People are just getting rid of their cable connection and getting TV in other ways. It is a disruptive force because when taken to its limit, it can kill the cable business. It has made it harder for cable companies to keep raising prices.

"

A force that pushes a firm towards disruption is a disruptive force. These include many competitive, environmental, socio-economic and behavioral changes.

GoogleDocs is another such example where users can get a free office productivity suite online. Users have been adopting Google Docs in place of the traditional Microsoft Office. It has made it harder for Microsoft to continue its lucrative upgrade cycle.

Disruption is the End of the Road That Few Reach

Disruption as the displacement of an incumbent is the end of a painful road that most firms never reach. Most large and powerful incumbents survive in the face of disruptive forces. But, they go through massive pain.

I have met with leaders of businesses facing disruptive forces going through massive pain on a daily basis. They miss a quarter here, are unable to provide opportunities to employees there. Sometimes they have no option but to lay off employees. Although their business would not get disrupted, they face enormous pain.

Mistakes Incumbent Managers Make

Most businesses will experience disruptive forces, but few will get disrupted. That is a reality. That means you should worry more about disruptive forces than disruption. There is also another reason why you should do so.

In my research, I found managers often underestimate the probability of disruption. There are deeply rooted psychological biases at play that make managers overconfident. This means that they often take the threats less seriously, believing their business is safe from disruption.

The bottom line is that if you think of disruption as a binary event, you are likely going to underestimate the probability of disruption. It may make you overlook the power of a disruptive force and the pain it would cause you as well as your business.

Instead, if you think of a disruptive force as a non-binary force, you are less likely to underestimate its power. Although something may not disrupt your business, it can still cause you significant pain. In that scenario, you are less likely to ignore that threat.

Conceptualizing Disruption

My prescription is to move away from thinking about disruption as a binary event. Think of it as a force rather than an end; it's a journey. Think of it as shades of gray rather than black and white.

When you consider disruptive forces on a spectrum of weak to strong, you will respond the way you should. You will take each of these disruptive forces for what they are. You will see them as forces that can cause you a range of painful experiences. Then you are less likely to ignore or overreact. Then you will be ready to deal with disruptive forces.

> **"**
> My prescription is to move away from thinking about disruption as a binary event. Think of it as a force rather than an end.

♀ CHAPTER INSIGHT:

How many disruptive forces have you identified in your industry?

A SIXTY-MINUTE GUIDE TO DISRUPTION
DR. ANKUSH CHOPRA

CHAPTER VII:
CAN YOU PREDICT DISRUPTION?

Often, managers wonder if it is possible to predict disruption. This is a frequent concern given how popular the term disruption has become. If you understand the drivers that lead to disruption, can you also predict disruption?

Theoretically speaking, you can point to the conditions needed for disruption. However, it is hard to predict disruption because firms can determine their fate with their actions and choices. As a result, a firm may face a disruptive forces but avoid being disrupted.

For a disruption to take place two things need to happen. First, the forces maintaining status quo need to change. Second, the incumbents have to be unable to respond to such change. Most people only look at the first condition when predicting disruption. That is a mistake.

" For a disruption to take place, two things need to happen.

Predicting Change in an Industry

To predict change in an industry, you can start by understanding the forces that maintain status quo. This understanding will help you point to potential changes in a systematic manner.

I developed a cascading change model that that explains what protects existing profits and maintains status quo in an industry. Although I have explained this framework in great detail in Chapter 2 of my book *The Dark Side of Innovation,* it is a useful model to recap here. As long as the forces that preserve industry profits remain in equilibrium, status quo continues.

I conceptualized four forces that protect profits in any industry. Using the example of the car-for-hire business, let me explain these four forces.

The Four Cs of status quo

1. Consumer and industry paradigm

It is acceptable that using a taxi to travel is a worthwhile activity. As a result, there are cabs and cab users in the world. For personal transportation, it is a common way to travel short distances. This forms a broad worldview within which the industry exists.

2. Consumer norms and routines

It is accepted that you can hail a cab on the road or call one using a phone. The alternatives include limo service, buses and trains. For personal transportation, renting a car or hiring a taxi are two options people often consider. These norms allow buyers and suppliers to exist and transact with each other in predictable ways.

3. Capabilities of suppliers

To serve consumer needs, many companies created car rental businesses. Similarly, many firms also operated taxis. As a result, these companies built a set of capabilities that enabled them to serve the customers. These capabilities included fleet management and customer service. These capabilities allowed firms to serve customers in an efficient and effective manner.

4. Consumption bundles

People either rented a car for a day or used a cab. These were the consumption bundles. They arise as pre-packaged units of value transacted between buyers and sellers.

You can think of these four Cs as cascading forces that maintain status quo. If you think of each of the forces as concentric circles with the paradigm as the outermost circle and the consumption bundle as the inner most circle, you can see why I call them cascading changes.

For a disruption to occur, one of these four must change in a major way. In the car-for-hire business, new firms with new capabilities arrived on the scene. Uber brought a way of using underutilized spare capacity in private cars. Zipcar brought the ability to rent a car by the hour. These two changes in service offerings led to a change in the consumer norms and routines. People could use an app to get an Uber or use Zipcar to rent a car. This allowed for a change in the consumer routines.

" When the four Cs in cars for hire industry change significantly, conditions for disruption arise.

When one of the four Cs in cars-for-hire industry change significantly, conditions for disruption will arise. But if these changes affect only a small part of the business, they would not lead to disruption.

You can use this framework to understand disruptive forces in any industry. The digital camera was a new consumption bundle that required new capabilities for camera makers. It led to a change in consumer norms of not needing film or photofinishing. It also changed the paradigms around when and how often to take pictures. This new technology created a massive change in the industry (which is a precondition for disruption).

Sometimes, disruption can start from a change in norms. For example, watching television and reading the news over the internet are new behaviors becoming normal.

Earlier and into the mid-twentieth century, people used cable or over-the-air TV and print newspapers. At that time, content distributors controlled the content; that is how they made money. But with the recent abundant access to the Internet, content consumers have many more choices of news outlets. Traditional content distributors do not control much of the competing content. As a result, the "older" news information distributors need to adapt to this change. Without adaptation, they will not be able to survive in an age of dwindling profits.

In this example, a change in norms set up cascading changes in the four pillars. This led to preconditions for disruption.

Inadequate Incumbent Response

No matter what changes the status quo, as long as incumbents can adapt to that change there won't be any disruption.

An incumbent will only get disrupted if it does not adapt to a change in its industry. Kodak was not disrupted because the industry changed massively; rather, it was disrupted because of an inadequate response to digital camera threat.

> **"**
> No matter what changes the status quo, as long as incumbents can adapt to that change there won't be any disruption.

When search behavior on the internet moved from desktop to mobile, it was a change in status quo. Google adapted to that change and thus there was no disruption for Google.

Video consumption moved from physical discs to consuming streaming video over the internet. But Netflix responded in a way that it continued to serve the customer in the new world. As a result, Netflix did not face disruption.

Currently, Uber and Lyft are aggressively moving into the self-driving car space. If the companies create or adapt to this new technology then they will survive; otherwise, they may get disrupted.

Only if the incumbents are unable to respond do they fall behind and get disrupted.

Why Disruption is Hard

The four Cs change slowly and often give enough notice to watchful incumbents. Furthermore, dominant corporations are more likely to respond to changes in status quo than not. This makes disrupting an industry difficult.

There is another reason why disruption is hard. I found this in my research as well as in research done by many others. Established firms often get a lot of leeway in responding to disruptive threats. Due to their brands, channels and customer relations, they get a "second wind" more often than not. Even when they struggle to respond, they do not automatically get disrupted.

Yet, there are some challenges that incumbents find difficult to handle. I also discovered while conducting research that cognitive biases often create barriers for incumbents. Due to these barriers, incumbents often do not respond adequately to a change in their industry. Most of this ensues because the incumbents underestimate the threat they face. Due to their complacency, they lose time and fall prey to a disruptor's strategy. (You can learn more about these cognitive challenges by downloading a free introductory chapter of **my book from my website ankushchopra.com**.)

> **"**
> One can only point to conditions that could lead to disruption, but the fate of incumbents is decided by the leaders of firms.

In short, although one can point to the conditions that could lead to disruption, the fate of incumbents is decided by the leaders of those firms. Sometimes companies are unable to adapt to minor changes and get disrupted, whereas at other times firms overcome huge odds and continue to survive in spite of massive changes in an industry. We saw why firms often find it hard to adapt to changes in chapter 2 earlier.

💡CHAPTER INSIGHT:

What do you fear more in your industry? The emerging conditions for disruption or your inability to respond to them?

CHAPTER VIII:
WHY DO SOME BUSINESS MODELS BECOME DISRUPTIVE?

Most often, people think of technology as a disruptor. However, by now you know that anything that causes a change in the industry can cause disruption. On this line of thinking, it is important to understand why some business models disrupt whereas others don't. Why did Netflix disrupt Blockbuster but Zipcar did not disrupt the car rental industry? Why did AirBNB not disrupt the hotel industry?

Considering answers to "why" can help you assess the threat of new business models in your industry. You can then respond in a thoughtful manner.

The Mechanism of Business Model Disruption

For a business model to become disruptive, it must do two things.

Replace Existing Demand

First, the new business model has to substitute an existing business model in the market. When Netflix offered video rental by mail, it didn't create a new market or segment the old market. Customers began to replace renting at the local store with renting online. In another example, Zipcar did not substitute the car rental market. Instead, it created a new market for rent by the hour, which did not exist earlier. It did take a small share from the traditional car rental firms but did not replace the market demand.

A new model substitutes an old model usually because it provides the same value but does it better. As a result, it places a newcomer firm at an advantage over incumbents.

> **"**
> A new model substitutes an old model usually because it provides the same value but does it better.

The Netflix business model replaced the traditional model. By centralizing the inventory, it increased movie choices and eliminated the cost of stores. This placed Netflix at a major advantage over Blockbuster.

Prevent Incumbents from Embracing New Models

The other requirement for a disruption is that the incumbents should not embrace the new business model. If an incumbent can easily embrace the new business model, it would not suffer a disruption. You may see a parallel with mechanisms of disruption here. When new business models replace an existing one, it creates a change in the industry. The inability to embrace the new model is an inability to adapt to that change.

When Apple brought apps to mobile devices, it threatened Google's search business. Google embraced the mobile paradigm with its Android platform and enhanced mobile search. It became more dominant in mobile search.

Similarly, Netflix and Hulu began selling video content on subscription over the internet. Consumers could watch shows on any device at home or on the go. The viewers valued this feature as well as lower costs and began cutting the cord. However, cable companies emulated some of the benefits such as streaming ability. There has been no disruption of incumbents due to these new models.

"
> But often a new business model prevents companies from embracing it. That is when disruption takes place.

But often a new business model prevents companies from embracing it. That is when disruption takes place. Three critical reasons contribute to the inability of incumbents to embrace new models:

Rigidities

Sometimes existing activity systems prevent incumbents from embracing new models. Blockbuster could not adopt the new business model in a costless manner. It would have had to sell its stores and lay off thousands of people. It was not easy to do that.

At other times, existing contracts and reliance on partners create other rigidities. When Dell created a direct-to-consumer model in the PC industry, the incumbents could not embrace it. The incumbents relied on their resellers for all sales. By embracing the new model, they would have started competing with their resellers. This could have resulted in boycotts by resellers. As a result, resellers created a rigidity for the incumbents.

Loss of Competitive Advantage

If an incumbent loses its competitive advantage by adopting a new model, it will hesitate to make that commitment. Walmart has a strong competitive advantage from the rural presence of its stores. If it embraces the online platform, it will dilute its competitive advantage. At the same time, it will compete in an area where Amazon has a stronger competitive advantage. In such situations, an existing competitive advantage prevents firms from embracing new models. This is why Walmart decided to buy jet.com to compete with Amazon. It is too early to say how this acquisition will turn out for Walmart.

Economic Rationale

Sometimes, there is just not enough profit in the new model and thus it makes no sense to adopt it. Index funds heralded a business model where profits were lower than in previous models. It made it harder for incumbents to embrace the new business model.

These three reasons can prevent incumbents from embracing new business models. Often these rigidities put the incumbents in a situation where they need to choose between a rock and a hard place. If this seems an impossible scenario, you must remember that many firms have succeeded against such odds in the past. I will share some examples of firms who succeeded in similar situation and will detail a method to deal with such situations.

" If you see new models emerge, you must ask two questions to assess whether they are disruptive or not.

DR. ANKUSH CHOPRA

If you see new models emerge you must ask two questions to assess whether they are disruptive or not. First, will the new model substitute the existing model? Second, will you find some major rigidity that will prevent you from embracing the new model? If the answer to both the questions is yes, then you are looking at a potentially disruptive business model.

💡 CHAPTER INSIGHT:

Are new business models in your industry disruptive or benign?

CHAPTER IX:
HOW MINOR INNOVATIONS CAN DISRUPT

Disruption of firms happen due to major innovations, right? Digital cameras disrupted Kodak. Cars disrupted horse and buggy companies. Quartz watches disrupted mechanical watchmakers. These were major innovations that led to disruption of incumbents.

Disruption by Minor Innovations

You may be surprised to know that incremental innovations can also cause disruption.

I studied the history of CT scanner industry when conducting research on innovation by established firms. I found incremental innovations were responsible for more disruptions than could be attributed to major innovations. I also found that a disruptive innovation didn't always disrupt the incumbents.

“

> I found incremental innovations were responsible for more disruptions than major innovations.

CT Scanners as a Major Innovation

CT scanner technology is a result of combining X-ray technology with algorithms. It was a major breakthrough. It could provide a tomographic image (an image of a cross section) of

DR. ANKUSH CHOPRA

a body rather than a super imposed image that was typically created from an x-ray. A CT scan allows you to see what you would see in a slice of a body if you actually cut it, utterly impossible before the CT scanner arrived on the scene.

When customers went to buy a CT scanner versus an X-ray machine, they were looking at new criteria: can the machine look inside a body without invasive surgery? This was not possible with an X-ray machine. Since the innovation changed the purchase criteria, it was a disruptive technology.

A Newcomer Takes Over the Market

Before the arrival of CT scanners, GE and Picker dominated the X-ray market. EMI, an outsider to the x-ray market, brought CT imagery as a potentially disruptive technology. GE and Picker struggled to create their own CT scanners in the first five years. As a result, EMI became the leader in the CT scanner market while GE and Picker watched from the sidelines.

GE and Picker struggled because they did not understand the algorithm technology in CT scanners. It took them several years to learn it. During that time, EMI continued to be a leader.

Incremental Innovation Race Begins

Within five years, both GE and Picker had launched their own scanners. At that time, the industry had begun a race to build a better scanner. Better scanners meant higher resolution and higher speeds. As various participants began to improve the scanners, a lot of "give and take" occurred in market share. Each player incrementally improved its products. Within the second five years of the technology's existence, both GE and Picker had improved their technologies to surpass that of EMI.

The Pioneer Falls Off the Cliff

As EMI fell behind in the technology, it also fell behind in market share. As a result, EMI found it harder and harder to compete with GE and Picker. It exited the CT scanner market within 12 years of creating the highly lucrative market. This is a stark example of disruption by incremental innovations.

> **"**
> This was a stark example of disruption by incremental innovations.

The Case of Apple versus Blackberry and Symbian

Although the CT scanner story is from the 70s, it has been repeated in many industries. Disruption by incremental innovations takes place often. We just fail to register it. In the recent past, Apple shook the smartphone market with its iPhone; it led to disruption of Symbian and Blackberry. Instead of one major innovation, Apple came out with many minor innovations.

> **"**
> Disruption by incremental innovations takes place often. We just fail to register it.

Symbian was a dominant leader in the smartphone OS with half the world's market share while Blackberry held over 20% market share. Apple improved the smartphone OS with a better browser and a touchscreen. These two incremental innovations led to a drastic decline of Symbian and Blackberry, causing them to lose their dominant positions.

Blackberry and Symbian continued to improve their operating

systems, but could not catch up with the incremental innovations of Apple. They lost their dominant position in the industry. In early 2009, Symbian and Blackberry controlled 70% of the market, but three years later, their combined market share was 15%. iPhone was a major reason for this disruption.

The race between Apple and Google is also worth noting. Anticipating an existential threat from Apple, Google entered the smartphone fray early on. It created a rival operating system for smartphones and began to give it away virtually free to hardware makers. The two companies competed with incremental innovations over time. Google's OS was virtually free, making it a significantly better value for numerous smartphone makers. Lower prices helped drive android OS towards dominance. Apple continued to hold its position against a rival who was giving away its operating system for free.

There is a lot more to the smartphone story than I have shared but given my goal of creating a short and easy to digest book, more details just didn't fit here.

Disruption in the smartphone market was primarily led by incremental innovations, but caused significant pain for the former dominant market leaders.

♀CHAPTER INSIGHT:

Do you look at the cadence of innovation as a driver of disruption in your industry?

CHAPTER X:
ARE SOME INDUSTRIES MORE PRONE TO DISRUPTION?

Given that several industries are facing disruptive forces, it's normal to wonder if your business is vulnerable to disruption. This can be framed as a broader question: are some industries more prone to disruption than others? From an incumbent's perspective, this is an existential question. Even from a disruptor's perspective, this is a critical issue.

Mapping Conditions for Disruption

As mentioned in Chapter 7, two conditions are critical for a disruption in any market. First, there has to be a massive change in the status quo. Second, the incumbents have to be unable to respond to this shift.

Two Conditions Critical for Disruption

Change refers to a change in a company's environment that makes the company less relevant. For example, when electric cars dominate the market, an incumbent who doesn't sell electric cars will be at a disadvantage. At the same time, change doesn't threaten an incumbent who can adapt to that change. As pointed out in earlier chapters, when web search moved to mobile devices, Google was able to adjust to that change. That change didn't lead to a disruption for Google.

Disruption Map

Using these two conditions, we can draw a two by two matrix of the world of business. The horizontal axis represents the magnitude of change taking place in an industry. The vertical axis represents the degree of management agility or the ability of a company to adapt to change.

The bottom right box is where most disruption would take place. This is where the degree of change is high and management agility is low. In such situations, conditions are ripe for disruption.

The top right box is also relevant. It refers to fast changing industries with high management agility. Disruption is possible there, but only because of management missteps. Let's go a bit deeper to identify what kind of companies in which kind of markets are easier to disrupt.

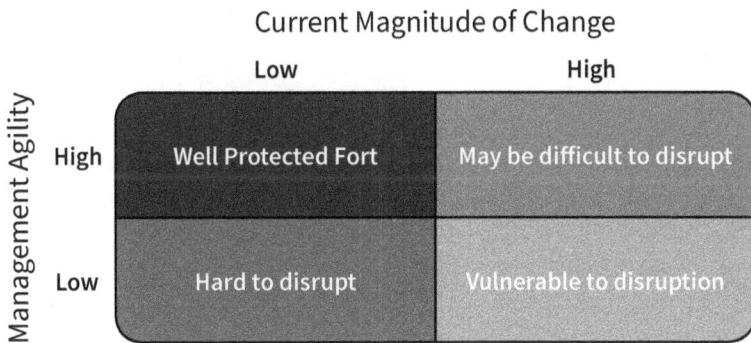

Current Magnitude of Change

	Low	High
High	Well Protected Fort	May be difficult to disrupt
Low	Hard to disrupt	Vulnerable to disruption

Management Agility

Drivers of Change

Industry change can be modeled in many different ways. I have detailed one model in my book, *The Dark Side of Innovation*. I also covered it in chapter seven on predicting disruption. There, I conceptualized the drivers of status quo in a cascading change model within an industry. Let's revisit that model using an example of photography market.

1. Paradigms

At a broad level, an industry emerges and exists due to paradigms of consumers. For example, 'taking pictures is a way of preserving memories' is a paradigm. The camera industry exists within this paradigm. Customers and suppliers emerge within this paradigm.

2. Norms

The buyers and suppliers follow some norms that provide a second level of stability in the industry. For example, film roll and camera constitute a product bundle that was commonplace to buy and sell. Using photofinishing services was another norm in the industry. On the supplier side, it was normal to expect that most of the profits are made in consumables like the film roll.

3. Capabilities

The third level of stability arises from the supplier capabilities that develop over time. These skills refer to key strengths that vendors develop while serving the customers.

Kodak developed three skills over time: chemical capabilities, brand, and a distribution network. These capabilities prevented new entry to the industry. DuPont tried to enter the film industry but wasn't able to compete with Kodak. Kodak's superior chemical capabilities prevented DuPont from establishing a position.

These capabilities allow firms to efficiently and effectively serve the consumers. This results in sticky buyer-supplier relationships and predictable transactions in an industry.

4. Offerings

Finally, the products and services being offered provide the fourth level of stability. Film rolls, cameras, and photofinishing services were a part of the product offering in the industry.

These consumption bundles prevent buyers and suppliers from rethinking consumption bundles on a going basis. Predictability, habits and expectations create a web of interactions that maintain the status quo.

As these four pillars of stability remained constant, the industry witnessed a status quo. When they changed, it led to an industry change.

In the case of Kodak, the product offerings changed and required a change in capabilities of competitors. Sony came up with a digital camera that needed no film to capture and store pictures. Kodak needed to build new electronics skills. This change also led to other changes in norms and paradigms.

People began to take pictures where they didn't take pictures before the innovation. Images of documents and business cards replaced faxes. Sharing of images became new norms. Pictures as a communication medium became a new paradigm.

These led to a massive change in the photography industry.

Management Agility

The ability to respond to change is often a result of how much change a company has experienced in the past. If you have experienced a massive change in a recent period, you are more agile and vice versa.

Handling change is also a management capability. It encompasses much more than processes and management information systems. It also requires agility of the mind of managers. Cognitive rigidities are often harder to overcome than process and information system rigidities.

A company in an industry that has seen little change for an extended period is less likely to have an agile management team. But, a business in a fast changing industry is more likely to have a flexible leadership. Therefore, companies buffered by strong brands, consistent paradigms, hard-bound technologies and well-established norms may have less agile management.

“

Cognitive rigidities are often harder to overcome than process and information system rigidities.

Insurance, banking and consumer goods are some examples of industries that have not seen much change for a long time. Companies in these industries will find it harder to deal with change. But, enterprise software, hardware and networking industries all have seen a lot of changes. Companies that have survived in these industries are more likely to have more agile managements.

DR. ANKUSH CHOPRA

Areas Vulnerable to Disruption

Does this mean that disruption in Insurance will be easier than in operating systems? To some extent, this is true. Dollar Shave Club could quickly take more than eight percent of the market in shave care because the industry had seen little change for a long time. Although Gillette was well versed in technology and innovation, it was not well versed with business model changes. Similarly, Betterment and Wealthfront have had early success in investment management because the industry had not seen much change.

However, this does not mean that changing industry will always lead to disruption. The challenge for a disruptor is different in the two right boxes from the earlier graph. In industries such as consumer goods, the challenge is to bring about a change in the industry. Adding technology to products that have had little technology is the most obvious path to disruption in such sectors.

❝
> However, this does not mean that changing industry will always lead to disruption.

For example, ebooks injected technology into a sleepy industry of book publishing and retailing. Although disruption may be easier in such sectors, the ability to bring about change is hard because it requires new-to-the-world technologies.

At the same time, digitization is the common trend where technology is being injected into previously low-tech areas. Toothbrushes with smartphone apps and Internet of things are two examples of digitization trends bringing about massive changes in hitherto slow moving industries.

On the other hand, disruption in fast moving industries would require either missteps by incumbents or more radical changes in the industry than what incumbents are used to seeing.

We know that Microsoft made a few missteps in handling the emergence of the Internet, and that led to an upheaval in the office productivity segment. It was a larger than normal change for Microsoft.

Sweet Spot for the Disruptor

Disruption can take place where the pace of change is high, so some industries may be easier to disrupt than others. But if the management is agile, it can prevent disruption. The sweet spot for a disruptor is where a disruptor can affect industry change and the management of incumbents is not agile.

♀CHAPTER INSIGHT:

Where does your business fit in the disruption map?

CHAPTER XI:
A DISRUPTION CASE STUDY
OF KODAK AND POLAROID

Kodak is the best poster child of disruption and a great case study on what can go wrong when a firm does not respond to a disruptive event adequately.

The Pioneer of Film Roll

Kodak was a pioneer of film-roll photography, ruling the industry for literally one hundred years. Kodak had garnered over 80% market share by the 1970s. Its success was due to its innovations in photographic film.

Before film roll, photography was a cumbersome process best left to experts. The process involved using glass plates coated with chemicals to get a picture exposure. But, the film roll changed the industry forever. Kodak placed the film camera in the hands of consumers and made it simpler to take pictures. It led to a rapid increase in camera and film sales.

Dominant Position

A key driver of Kodak's profits was the film roll; it yielded margins upwards of 60-70%. With a dominant market share and huge margins, Kodak was a cash machine. That is until digital cameras emerged.

> **"**
> With a dominant market share and huge margins, Kodak was a cash machine.

The Digital Camera Arrives

In the early 1980s, Sony announced a digital camera that needed no film. When a new technology appears in an industry, it could be a major threat as well as a significant opportunity. Often, it is not easy to assess the implications of such technologies early on. Smart companies keep scanning their environment for such technologies and react to them in a thoughtful manner. Kodak did what any smart company would do. It began learning the technology involved in a digital camera.

Kodak's Response

Kodak began to investigate the technology in earnest. It invested billions of dollars over the next ten years. Since the technology was new and underdeveloped, consumer acceptance was hard to achieve. This slow diffusion rate gave Kodak almost 20 years to be ready with its camera.

> **"** Kodak played to win in the digital imaging industry.

Kodak set up a research and development lab in Japan tasked with the goal to learn microelectronics. It set up a separate division that focused entirely on digital products, creating dozens of them. The most important product it developed was the imaging sensor. The sensor became the industry standard.

Above all, Kodak hired the ex-Motorola CEO George Fisher to transform the photography company into a hardware company. Kodak played to win in the digital imaging industry.

The Result

With those lofty goals and deep pockets, it's shocking to see the results of those efforts. By 2008, twenty-five years after the digital camera technology appeared on the market, Kodak had only 20% market share in the US digital camera industry. Its revenues declined from $20 billion in 1992 to $12 billion in 2008. Its profits declined from $1.2 billion in 1992 to $400mm in 2008. Eventually, it filed for bankruptcy.

The Reason for Disruption of Kodak

The problem with the digital camera technology was that it was a profit destroying innovation. Such innovations create cognitive challenges for incumbents, where companies often underestimate the disruptive power of such changes.

Digital cameras eliminated the need for film, thus led to the elimination of the most profitable part of the business for market leaders. In this sense, it was a profit-destroying innovation. Kodak was left with two choices: embrace the technology (which deliberately destroys its own profits) or avoid the technology in order to protect existing position.

I found in my research that when faced with these choices, firms often choose not to cut their own profits. This often leads to their decline.

In the 1980s, many observers predicted that digital camera would be the future of photography. As a result, Kodak took the threat seriously and invested in the technology.

Closer to the launch of its digital cameras, internal resistance to the innovation increased. Managers began questioning the rationale of replacing a high-profit product with a low-profit product because they realized that digital cameras would lead to a reduction in profits. The internal resistance had Kodak's sales people pointing customers towards analog cameras instead of digital cameras.

During this time, the digital imaging group was working on a large number of digital products. These included Kodak CD, Kodak CD player and others. The CD player was priced at $499. But consumers didn't see the point in converting their film rolls into CDs to watch on TV, so these products didn't succeed in the market.

The internal resistance was the key reason for the dismal performance of Kodak. Although it had developed the needed technology and had the most valuable patents, it still failed. The core reason was its inability to gauge the real threat from digital innovation. Kodak eventually filed for bankruptcy in 2011.

Polaroid's Reaction

The same reactions emerged at Polaroid, too. Polaroid owned 10% of the market due to its hold on instant photography. Polaroid had even prevented Kodak from entering its segment for decades. It maintained its hold on the segment due to numerous patents and continued technological innovation.

"
When digital camera innovation emerged, Polaroid also invested in the technology the way Kodak did.

When the digital camera innovation emerged, Polaroid also invested in the technology the way Kodak did. Closer to the launch, Polaroid met with similar internal resistance. Managers questioned why they should go into a 30% gross margin business that would replace a 70% gross margin business.

A SIXTY-MINUTE GUIDE TO DISRUPTION

DR. ANKUSH CHOPRA

This resistance was similar to what happened within Kodak.

The result was a delay in product launch and deliberate atrophy of excellent digital capabilities. In the end, Polaroid met with a similar fate as Kodak did – Polaroid went out of business through a bankruptcy filing in 2001.

A take away from the camera industry is that the incumbents did not ignore a disruptive force. They thought they were creating great options that would save their business. The mistake they made was to underestimate the power of a disruptive force.

What Kodak and Polaroid didn't do was also clear. They did not anticipate how their world would change. Instead, they assumed a future that would be benign to old technology cameras. They did not attempt to manage the disruptive force or respond to it in a systematic manner.

᛫CHAPTER INSIGHT

Does your company have a tsunami alert system that can highlight the tsunami of a disruptive force at distant horizons?

CHAPTER XII:
LIGHTING INDUSTRY FACING A DISRUPTIVE FORCE TODAY

The lighting industry has been facing a disruptive force for the last several years. It has some strong parallels with the history of the camera industry.

LED as a Disruptive Force

Light emitting diode (LED) technology provides long life lighting compared to the old bulb technology. As a result, the lighting industry will see a dramatic reduction in demand. Due to the long life of LED light, every LED light will eliminate the need for 25 incandescent bulbs. At the same time, the price of LED lighting has been declining.

Even if the lighting incumbents succeed in LED, they will still witness a drop in revenues. Their profits will fall too. At the same time, several new players such as Cree and Sharp have entered the lighting arena. These players pose the same challenge to the majors that consumer electronics majors such as Sony posed to Kodak and Polaroid.

Difficult Choices

When firms face the situation that Kodak and Polaroid faced, they are stuck with awful options. If they embrace the technology, they lose profits by eliminating their replacement demand. If they avoid the new technology, they may go out of business.

DR. ANKUSH CHOPRA

> **"** Research has shown that when decision makers face two choices that leave them worse off than status quo, they tend to avoid making the choice.

Research has shown that when decision makers face two choices that leave them worse off than the status quo, they tend to avoid making the choice. Kodak and Polaroid dragged their feet in the face of technologies that killed replacement demand. They found immense resistance within their organizations that stymied their commercialization efforts.

Furthermore, camera majors made some critical mistakes. They predicted a future based on their current capabilities. Kodak thought the future of the camera industry was a convergence between chemistry and microelectronics; it pursued such convergence products. Polaroid believed that the future of the camera was mini printers on top of digital cameras.

Both were deluding themselves. Both Polaroid and Kodak suffered disruption. Both also missed some key parallel trends, such as PC penetration and the rise of the Internet. These trends provided key value-creating opportunities upon which others could capitalize.

Important Implications

The lighting majors are facing intense competition from new players as other companies such as Sharp and Cree bring new capabilities to the market. Another key challenge for lighting majors will be the fact that the drivers of success will change. Currently, distribution, brand and pricing determine the profits of a firm.

In LED, technology and price will drive success. There will be a shakeout in the industry at some point. After the shakeout, technology will become less important (as often seen after shakeouts in such situations). This shakeout may lead to the exit of one or more current lighting majors, as has happened in many other industries in the past.

The lighting majors need to watch for the key cognitive challenges similar to those that camera majors faced. These problems arise from a set of heuristics that managers in any industry share.

Blurred Boundaries

The lighting majors will see a blurring of industry boundaries. As firms try to go beyond the socket, they may aim at opportunities both close to and far from the traditional industry boundaries.

Home automation, fixtures, data networking and services will all be up for grabs. The collective effort of firms will determine the new industry boundaries.

The path from here to there will also lead companies down some dead ends. Kodak's efforts on Kodak CD and CD players and Polaroid's efforts of placing a printer on top of digital cameras were examples of dead ends. The way to avoid dead ends is to "bust your blinders" that force a company to see the future through the rosy lens of its past success.

The Path for Disruptors

Although the going seems tough for the incumbents, Sharp and Cree will also not have an easy path. In the camera industry, while major players such as Kodak lost, many new entrants also lost. Apple, the legendary creator of the iPhone,

A SIXTY-MINUTE GUIDE TO DISRUPTION

DR. ANKUSH CHOPRA

entered the camera industry but failed to win. Although changing technology does open doors for new entrants, the road to victory is not an easy one.

The new entrants should note that none of the three lighting majors (GE, Philips, and Osram) are as dependent on the lighting industry as Kodak and Polaroid were reliant on the camera industry. This gives these lighting majors leeway that the camera majors didn't have.

The distribution channels will be an important aspect of this game for the first round; newcomers may find it challenging to fight majors in the distribution game. Newcomers should not forget how promising innovators in the camera industry, such as Apple and SMaL, could not succeed against the consumer electronics firms. But things have changed in the distribution landscape too. The internet as a great leveler may produce opportunities for new entrants in the lighting space.

Who Will Win the Future?

The lighting industry is an example of a major disruptive force is at play. The key challenges for incumbents are clear. Home Depot and Walmart are already carrying many new LED brands. The outcome will depend on how the lighting majors manage disruption.

♀CHAPTER INSIGHT:

Do you see parallels to this case in any segment of your industry?

CHAPTER XIII:
POTENTIAL SWISS WATCH DISRUPTION 2.0

After looking at the past disruption of Kodak, an ongoing disruption in the lighting industry, let's examine a potential disruption. Although the Swiss watch industry underwent disruption in the 1970s, it may be disrupted again. This is a consideration making the rounds among the industry participants and observers.

Back in the 1970s, the Swiss watch industry faced massive losses in its global position due to the quartz technology; smartwatches may do the same to the wristwatch industry.

"

> Is this an opportunity for industry leaders to use lessons learned in the disruptive wave of the 1970s?

Should the watchmakers adopt a smartwatch technology or deal with this threat in some other way? This question merits a longer answer than a simple prescriptive answer. This is also an opportunity for the industry leaders to think back about the lessons from the disruptive wave in the industry back in the 1970s.

The Original Swiss Watch Industry Disruption

The Swiss watch industry faced disruption in the 1970s when the quartz technology decimated the industry in a short span of ten years. Over half of the firms in the industry disappeared, and more than half of the employees lost their jobs during that time.

The problem back then was not that the Swiss watch industry faced a disruptive force in quartz technology; the problem was how the Swiss watchmakers reacted to that disruptive force. (A longer narrative on this historic event is included in *The Dark Side of Innovation*.)

How Swatch Overcame Disruptive Forces

In the midst of that carnage, a single firm (Swatch) demonstrated how companies could overcome massive disruptive forces with a creative strategy. The lessons from Swatch are still pertinent, and the global watch industry needs to heed those lessons at this time. Swatch redefined what a watch was and therein lay the secret to its successful response. Watchmakers need to go down a similar path rather than just think of whether to adopt smart watches or avoid the technology altogether.

Thinking About Watches

Consider what is a watch? Obviously, it is a time keeping device, but there is more to it. In the beginning, pocket watches used to be the time keeping devices and wristwatches appeared much later; eventually, wrist watches became the dominant design of a watch.

The watch moved from being just a timekeeping device to being a piece of jewelry. Along with this change, the watch as a time keeping device appropriated the wrist real estate. The quartz revolution only solidified the wrist as the natural real estate for watches.

> **"**
> In essence, the watch is a true owner of the wrist real estate, and that is the critical asset of wrist watchmakers.

However, with the advent of cell phones, the time keeping function moved from the wrist to a mobile device that was often kept in a pocket; the timekeeping device moved back to the pocket.

Although the primary time keeping device moved from the wrist to the cell phone, wristwatches remained the natural heirs of the wrist real estate. This was because of the association of watches with wrist real estate in the minds of consumers. This makes the wrist a critical asset for the wrist watchmakers.

Smart Watches and the Battle for the Wrist

Since the advent of health devices (such as Fitbit and smart watches like the Apple Watch), a battle for the wrist real estate has been going on. Obviously, smart watches and health monitoring devices are in no way comparable to watches. Nevertheless, they are perceived as somewhat related to a wrist watch due to their design as well as the real estate they are trying to occupy (the wrist). In essence, the fight between the wrist watchmakers and the smart watch makers is not about technology or branding or benefits – it is a battle of the wrist real estate.

In one scenario, the smart watch could abandon the wrist and move to the real estate naturally occupied by glasses (like Google Glass). While watchmakers may pray for this outcome, as of today, the real estate eyed by the smart devices is the wrist. As a result, the watchmakers need a response, and they need it fast.

> **"** The fact that this is a battle of the wrist between the watch makers and the smart watch makers points to a novel insight.

The fact that this is a battle of the wrist happening between the watch makers and the smart watch makers points to a novel insight. From one perspective, watchmakers are under threat from smart watch makers; the threat is that smart watches will usurp the natural real estate of watch makers. At the same time, this also appears to be an opportunity to occupy a greater share of the wrist real estate. The wrist can be seen as a pivot point for watchmakers. It could be a beachhead to broaden their arena.

Understanding New Capabilities

Watchmakers are known for their aesthetics, design, brands and their ability to make their customers feel great with an elegant piece of jewelry. Smart watch makers are known for their software and extensive functionality in a mobile device. When viewed from the smart watch makers' perspective, they lack some of the critical capabilities that traditional watchmakers possess; the same applies for the traditional watchmakers who know almost nothing about software and operating system platforms.

The threat to watchmakers is that if they totally adopt the smart watch core into their watches, their competitive advantage may be significantly eroded. On the other hand, a direct battle with devices may be a losing battle for the traditional watchmakers.

Designing a Response to Disruptive Threat

The key to a robust response will be how to provide smart watch features along with the benefits of the traditional watches: the million dollar feeling of wearing a great piece of jewelry. There are many solutions and depending on the exact capabilities and resources of a watchmaker, there needs to be a personalized strategic response to this existential threat. This would require not just new capabilities, but a new thinking, new ways of looking at the world and organizing for this new world.

No Obvious Answers

Lest it appears that all that is needed is to add a smart watch core to a traditional watch, one should not forget that Sony tried to do exactly this and the outcome was not pretty.

Sony was a traditional hardware company that faced competition from new devices that incorporated software as a critical core. Sony created a software division to provide software in devices. However, the glorious history of hardware success made the software engineers get the short end of the stick at Sony. As a result, in spite of significant resources expended on software, the launches were mired with problems.

66

The next Swatch in Switzerland will have to be a master of disruption management.

The cause of the problem for Sony was that it thought adding a software division is all that it needed. There was a lot more that was needed to transform a hardware company to a software based hardware company.

The next Swatch company for the Swiss watchmakers will be the company that not only figures out the product solution, but also figures out how to organize to deliver such a product. Such a company will indeed be a master of disruption management.

♀ CHAPTER INSIGHT

How are you searching for answers to disruptive forces in your industry?

CHAPTER XIV:
WINNING AGAINST DISRUPTIVE FORCES: THE CASE OF DE BEERS

People often overestimate the power of disruptive forces when the company being disrupted is not their own. In fact, many people believe that a disruptive force will always crush incumbents. However, this is not the case. In fact, companies often crush disruptive forces that arise in their industries.

" Companies often crush disruptive forces that arise in their industries.

The Case of De Beers

One of the best examples of a company that crushed a disruptive force is De Beers. It dominates and controls the world diamond market. A diamond is valuable because it is a rare material. By controlling the supply, De Beers was able to ensure the market remains profitable.

A Disruptive Force in the Diamonds Industry

Although diamond mines were the only source of diamonds since beginning of time, scientist have now figured out a way to produce diamonds in a laboratory. By simulating geological events in the laboratory, it became possible to manufacture a diamond. Chemically, it was no different from a mined diamond. Moreover, you could also play around with the four

Cs (color, cut, clarity and carat weight) of a diamond and thus create valuable diamonds.

These manufactured diamonds could flood the market. What would be the impact on De Beers if people began to see them the same way as mined diamonds? It would have destroyed the diamond industry in the way cultured pearls destroyed the pearls industry.

De Beers' Response

De Beers did two critical things to overcome this disruptive threat. First, It took legal action against the laboratory diamond makers. The courts ruled that such diamonds should be called synthetic diamonds. Second, it unleashed an intense marketing campaign to highlight the value of real diamonds. This approach allowed De Beers to crush the disruptive force in its industry. Its marketing blitz differentiated mined diamonds from synthetic diamonds in the eyes of consumers. It ensured people appreciated mined diamonds more.

This is how De Beers was able to overcome a major threat of disruption.

You Determine the Endgame of Disruption

The key lesson here is that even if a disruptive force is threatening your industry, you can respond to that threat in many ways. In fact, many firms have succeeded against disruptive forces. The De Beers' example is just one of the many strategies available to you to deal with disruptive forces. In the next chapter, you will find the three key ways to respond to a disruptive force in your industry.

💡CHAPTER INSIGHT

Are you feeling confident that you can win over disruptive forces in your industry?

CHAPTER XV:
HOW TO RESPOND TO DISRUPTIVE FORCES

Although disruptive forces are often challenging for incumbents, disruptors rarely get an easy pass. In fact, incumbents fight tooth and nail, often winning against disruptive forces. On the other hand, it is not uncommon for large and established companies to fall from their lofty positions in their industries.

Based on my research of hundreds of firms across dozens of industries, I found that incumbents use three sets of responses when faced with disruptive forces. These are not mutually exclusive and companies often use them in conjunction with each other.

Scuttle the Disruptive Force

When faced with disruptive forces, incumbents often resort to scuttling the disruptor or the disruptive force. Firms often use two methods to achieve this goal.

A. Legal Recourse

Using the legal route, incumbents sometimes try to scuttle the path forward for the disruptor. The aim here is often to stop the disruptor in its tracks using the force of law. Give how expensive it can be to pursue a legal course, sometimes disruptors have no option but to give in to the deep pockets of the incumbents.

This technique using the force of law involves demonstrating that the disruptor is using a patented technology or using pre-emptive patenting to prevent the competitor from moving forward.

A recent lawsuit by Gillette on Dollar Shave Club is an example where an incumbent tries to stop a disruptor by preventing it from using some of the allegedly patented technologies.

If you recall, in the early stage of intense fight between Apple and Google in smartphones, several lawsuits and counter-suits were filed by each against the other. In fact, Apple was becoming a big deterrent for Google. At that time, Google bought Motorola's mobility division for over $12 billion just for the patents that Motorola held. This was a cost for Google to just play in an industry where Apple held numerous critical patents.

At other times, firms use the law to make it harder for the disruptor. For example, De Beers launched a legal offensive against laboratory made diamonds so that they could not be sold as real diamonds. It won the legal fight, and this ensured that all laboratory made diamonds were called synthetic diamonds.

B. Consumer Based Offensive

The second route often involves convincing the customers that the product or service a disruptor is peddling is not the real thing. Alternately, it involves strengthening one's brand.

" The second route often involves convincing the customers that the disruptor is peddling fakes.

DeBeers not only used the legal route but also went on a massive advertising blitz to convince consumers that real diamonds are valuable and always hold value. It strengthened the equity of real diamonds in this campaign. As a result of De Beers' countermeasures to the disruptive forces, while the buyers valued real diamonds more, they also were made aware that real diamonds were different from synthetic diamonds.

Transform the Innovation

Although embracing a disruptive force is often hard to do because of one or more reasons, sometimes incumbents effectively embrace the innovation and move forward. Even when they are successful, it is not always easy to do this. Embracing a disruptive force is often easier for peripheral firms than the dominant firms.

Canon and Nikon adopted the digital technology and rode the wave of this disruptive force all the way to the leadership position in their industry. Since they didn't have to lose their existing investments and market position in film production, they found it easy to embrace the new technology. On the other hand, Kodak and Polaroid had a tough time embracing the technology, writing off their old investments and giving up strong market positions.

An effective response of the most successful firms facing disruptive forces has been to transform the innovation. When the Swiss watchmakers were collapsing under the threat of quartz technology, Swatch not only embraced the quartz technology but also transformed it. Instead of just selling Swiss-made quartz watches, it converted watches from time-keeping devices to fashion accessories.

> **"** Swatch not only embraced the threat of quartz, it also transformed it.

After the mutual fund industry faced the index fund threat, it eventually created exchange traded funds (ETFs) of different stripes. ETFs evolved into an enormous number of instruments thereby expanding the market. Some of these were quite lucrative because they targeted niche segments where investors were willing to pay a premium to access an idiosyncratic slice of the investment universe. Some of the ETFs had an active bent to them, which allowed firms to charge hefty fees even on ETFs.

Create New Value Streams

Often, it is not possible to either scuttle the disruptor or to transform the innovation. At such times, firms often rely on developing new value streams to ensure survival and continued strong position.

Some of the lighting majors are using this strategy. As light bulbs are being replaced by LED lighting, the total demand for lighting is declining. In this scenario, firms such as Philips and GE are looking at LED as the smart hub for the home. They are attempting to create new value streams from LED technology.

Opportunities for creating new value streams often arise as firms are forced to build new capabilities in the face of disruptive forces. LED technology is a new technology for lighting companies that could yield new business avenues such as smart home applications. Kodak was forced to learn microelectronics and it entered the printer business with new technologies.

The mistake that firms often make is to not anticipate the new capabilities they will need to develop ahead of time. As a result, they sometimes miss the opportunities to monetize new capabilities through careful planning.

The Three Pronged Antidote to Disruption

Firms have a number of options to deal with disruptive forces. Preventing emerging threats, transforming emerging threats and creating new revenue streams cover the entire gamut of strategies firms have. At the same time, it requires enormous creativity and grit to go through the process of designing an effective response.

💡 CHAPTER INSIGHT

Which of these three strategies are you actively considering in your response portfolio for disruptive forces?

READ MORE CASE STUDIES
ON DISRUPTION

The case of MUSIC INDUSTRY

Disruption in CLASSIFIEDS

The original SWISS WATCH DISRUPTION

Disruption in TAX PREPARATION SERVICES

Potential disruption in BLADES AND RAZORS INDUSTRY

PEARL INDUSTRY DISRUPTION

Go to the accompanying website and read an ever increasing collection of case studies, tools, and insights on disruption and innovation.

www.ankushchopra.com

CONCLUSION AND NEXT STEP:
YOU AND DISRUPTION

Today, we are in the age of disruption. Your business and your career are under threat from disruptive forces. Even if you think your business is safe, it only means that you have not yet identified the disruptive threats to your business.

A business facing a disruptive threat often has a demoralized workforce. Such companies find it difficult to provide career advancement to their employees.

Disruption as an Opportunity

Yet, if your business faces disruptive forces, you also have an enormous opportunity. If you are not the dominant player in the industry, this is a chance to become one. If you are the dominant player in your industry, it is a chance to secure your business in a new way for a long time. By mastering disruption, you can create a significant impact on your business and career.

A disturbing truth about the age of disruption is that managers across firms and at all levels are challenged by disruptive forces. At the same time, they have not been trained to deal with disruptive forces.

"

A disturbing truth about the age of disruption is that managers across firms and at all levels are challenged by disruptive forces.

DR. ANKUSH CHOPRA

The reason is two-fold. First, business schools are not teaching students how to manage disruption. Given how interdisciplinary and new this area is, schools do not have the needed knowledge and skills at this moment to teach this area. Second, since disruption historically was a rare phenomenon, firms do not have enough experience to deal with it. As a result, they have not learned the art of managing disruption.

The age of disruption gives you an immense opportunity to master this area and be at the forefront of new capabilities. By building skills in disruption management, you can be among the few who can claim to know this area. It will give you opportunities across industries and business areas.

Becoming A Disruptor

Becoming a disruptor is a significant step jump from becoming an innovator. If you consider the cascading change model I shared with you in earlier chapters, it shows you four paths to innovation. These four paths to innovation are:

1. Product or technology innovation: 4K technology in television is an example of a technology innovation

2. Capabilities innovation: Netflix provided a capability innovation in the video rental industry by bringing a new platform and logistics systems

3. Routines Innovation: Amazon brought a routines innovation by changing where and how people shop for books and other merchandise

4. Paradigm innovation: Microsoft brought about a paradigm innovation with its innovations around the PC. Microsoft changed the paradigm of what an office worker is and how and what she does

When an innovator brings about a change in an industry that incumbents are unable to adapt to, it leads to a disruption. As a result, a disruptor needs to be an innovator. The cascading change model shows that four different types of innovators exist.

By selecting industries and incumbents who will find it hard to respond to an innovation, an innvoator begins to evolve from being an innovator to being a disruptor. Here are a few resources to help you in your efforts to become a successful disruptor:

Read the Dark Side of Innovation

Having read this book is a great first step. You can go ahead and read my original book on disruption, **The Dark Side of Innovation**. Consider it the upper level tutorial to help you further master disruption. I detail psychological traps that managers hit when dealing with profit-destroying innovations. I also go into much more detail on how to design strategies to deal with disruption.

Visit the "Managing Disruption" Site

I have also created a disruption management area on my website where I continue to add new materials on a weekly basis. You can explore this **disruption management section**. Bookmark the page and visit it every week to know the latest on disruption.

*Visit: **http://ankushchopra.com/disruption-management/***

Join my Weekly Email Group

There is a lot more to disruption than covered in this book. By joining my weekly newsletter, you will get to know the latest works, insights, ideas, and tools. Reading my newsletter for two minutes a week will keep you updated on the latest in innovation and disruption management. This way, you can make sure you won't miss any of my latest articles.

*You can join the newsletter at **http://www.ankushchopra.com***

Join my Disruption Management Programs

I offer disruption management programs in the New York and Boston areas. If you are in these geographies, do inquire about how you can join my program. Send me an email to get more information on this program. You not only get to join me in-person to learn disruption but also get one-on-one coaching from me.

Seating is limited, and you need to be sponsored by your organization to join the program.

Have me Train Your Organization

I also train organizations on disruption management. A custom designed program built around your business maybe what you need today. I can help you develop and institute a process for managing disruption in your business.

*I hope you enjoyed reading this book and learned useful insights from it. If you have more questions please feel free to email me at **ankush@ankushchopra.com** I would love to hear from you.*

ABOUT THE AUTHOR

Dr. Ankush Chopra is an award winning author and professor. He is also the the founder and CEO of Epiphanies Etc Inc. The firm offers cutting edge innovation and strategy training programs for leading corporations. Disruption management is one of its flagship programs. You can find more information on the firm at www.epiphaniesetc.com

Chopra is a professor of Strategy at the School of Management, Fribourg. Fribourg is a beautiful town and canton in Switzerland. Prior to that, he was a professor of Strategy at Babson College for many years. His research focuses on making managers and organizations more effective innovators.

Chopra is the author of **The Dark Side of Innovation**, a book on how not to get disrupted in this age of disruption. The academic community acclaimed his research for this book. It received the best paper award by the International Conference on Innovation and Management. The paper was also published in the International Journal of Innovation in Management.

Prior to being an academic, Chopra had a successful managerial career at Procter & Gamble and Citibank. His deep desire to study innovation and strategy led him to pursue a Ph.D. He earned his Ph.D. from Duke University. He also has an MBA from Indian Institute of Management, Bangalore.

He has lived and worked in seven countries across three continents. These countries are India, Japan, Singapore, Philippines, UAE, Switzerland and the USA. He now lives with his family in the Greater New York area.

You can write to him at ankush@ankushchopra.com

SELECTED REFERENCES

Arthur, B. Increasing Returns and Path Dependence in the Economy. (1994). University of Michigan Press.

Chopra, A (2007) Inter-temporal Effect of Technological Capabilities on Firm Performance: a Longitudinal Study of the US Computed Tomography Industry (1972-2002), Ph.D. Dissertation

Chopra, A (2013) The Dark Side of Innovation. Brigantine Media.

Chopra, A., & Baldegger, R. (2015) Deer in the Headlights: Response of Incumbent Firms to Profit Destroying Innovations. International Journal of Innovation in Management.

Christensen, C. M. (1997) The innovator's dilemma: when new technologies cause great firms to fail. Harvard Business School Press.

King, A. A., & Tucci, C. L. (2002). Incumbent Entry into New Market Niches: The Role of Experience and Managerial Choice in the Creation of Dynamic Capabilities. Management Science, 48(2), 171.

Lepore, J (2014) The disruption machine. New Yorker. URL http://www.newyorker.com/magazine/2014/06/23/the-disruption-machine (Last accessed January 2017)

Schumpeter, Joseph A. (1994) [1942]. Capitalism, Socialism and Democracy. London: Routledge.

www.ingramcontent.com/pod-product-compliance
Lightning Source LLC
Chambersburg PA
CBHW031950190326
41519CB00007B/749